NEW VANGUARD • 157

LANDING CRAFT, INFANTRY AND FIRE SUPPORT

GORDON L ROTTMAN   ILLUSTRATED BY PETER BULL

First published in Great Britain in 2009 by Osprey Publishing,
PO Box 883, Oxford, OX1 9PL, UK
PO Box 3985, New York, NY 10185-3985, USA
Email: info@ospreypublishing.com

Osprey Publishing is part of the Osprey Group.

Transferred to digital print on demand 2014.

First published 2009
3rd impression 2011

Printed and bound by
Cadmus Communications, USA.

A CIP catalogue record for this book is available from the
British Library.

ISBN: 978 1 84603 435 0
PDF e-book ISBN: 978 1 84603 902 7

Page layout by Melissa Orrom Swan, Oxford
Index by Alan Thatcher
Typeset in Sabon and Myriad Pro
Originated by United Graphic Pte Ltd, Singapore

Acknowledgements

The author wishes to thank Denis Huff for providing LSM
photographs and Jimmy Prime, a former LCI(R) crewman, for
his insight.

The Woodland Trust

Osprey Publishing are supporting the Woodland Trust, the
UK's leading woodland conservation charity, by funding the
dedication of trees.

www.ospreypublishing.com

Abbreviations

amtrac	amphibious tractor (see LVT)
BuShips	Bureau of Ships
DUKW	"Duck" amphibious truck
HM	His Majesty's
hp	horsepower
kW	kilowatt
LCA	Landing Craft, Assault (RN)
LC(FF)	Landing Craft (Flotilla Flagship)
LCI(A)	Landing Craft, Infantry (Ammunition)
LCI(D)	Landing Craft, Infantry (Diver)
LCI(FS)	Landing Craft, Infantry (Fire Support)
LCI(G)	Landing Craft, Infantry (Gun)
LCI(H)	Landing Craft, Infantry (Headquarters)
LCI(L)	Landing Craft, Infantry (Large)
LCI(M)	Landing Craft, Infantry (Mortar)
LCI(R)	Landing Craft, Infantry (Rocket)
LCS(L)	Landing Craft, Support (Large)
LCT	Landing Craft, Tank
LCVP	Landing Craft, Vehicle and Personnel
LSI	Landing Ship, Infantry (RN)
LSM	Landing Ship, Medium
LSM(R)	Landing Ship, Medium (Rocket)
LSS(L)	Landing Ship, Support (Large)
LST	Landing Ship, Tank
LVT	Landing Vehicle, Tracked (amtrac)
RN	Royal Navy
STS	special treatment steel (armor)

Editor's note

For ease of comparison between types, Imperial/American
measurements are used almost exclusively throughout this
book. The following data will help in converting the
Imperial/American measurements to metric:

1 mile = 1.6km
1lb = 0.45kg
1yd = 0.9m
1ft = 0.3m
1in. = 2.54cm/25.4mm
1gal = 4.5 liters
1 ton (US) = 0.9 tonnes

CONTENTS

LANDING CRAFT, INFANTRY AND FIRE SUPPORT

"Protect me oh Lord for my boat is so small and your sea is so great."
From the Breton Fisherman's Prayer

INTRODUCTION

The Landing Craft, Infantry (Large) – LCI(L) – was a large beaching craft intended to transport and deliver an infantry rifle company to a hostile shore once the beachhead was secured, or as one soldier claimed: "The LCI was a metal box designed by a sadist to move soldiers across the water." The LCI and its larger vehicle-delivery counterpart, the Landing Ship, Medium (LSM), were important and widely used World War II amphibious-warfare ships. They were intermediate-size beaching craft, filling the gap between the much larger Landing Ship, Tank (LST)[1] and the many types of smaller, bow-ramped, open cargo compartment landing craft.

The LCI was strictly a passenger carrier and could not transport vehicles. Lacking bow doors or a ramp, cargo had to be hand-carried off the ship. The LCM, by contrast, could carry up to five tanks and other large vehicles as well as bulk cargo. It lacked the accommodation and sanitary facilities for large numbers of troops, other than for a short ship-to-shore haul. (Passenger accommodations were only for transported vehicle crews.)

The matter of designations as "craft" and "ship" must be addressed. Seagoing amphibious beaching vessels over 200ft in length were designated ships. The LSM was 203ft 6in long while the LCI(L) was 160ft. The LCI, nevertheless, was a seagoing vessel given moderate conditions and reasonable ranges. The type was redesignated Landing Ship, Infantry (LSI) on February 28, 1949, although few were still operational.

The LCI and LSM were the smallest landing vessels assigned Bureau of Ships (BuShips) hull numbers rather than names. Official names, for example, would be USS LCI(L)-351 or USS LSM-36. Those provided to the Royal Navy retained the US BuShips hull numbers, but were designated HM LCI(L)-2, for example (HM = His Majesty's). The Soviet Navy designated them "DS" (*desantnoye sudno* – assault ship) and assigned new numbers (e.g. DS.10), though they retained US hull numbers up until December 1945. To the sailors manning these awkward craft, they were known as the "Elsie Item" – "Elsie" representing "LC" and "Item" being the phonetic alphabet word for "I." Their boxy shape also led to their being called the "Floating Bedpan," perhaps influenced by the close troop quarters and limited toilet facilities, while destroyer crews working with them as radar pickets called them "small boys."

In 1943/44, the LCI and LSM both provided the hulls for new types of rocket-firing gunboats, known as "bazooka boats." Another type based on

1 See Osprey New Vanguard 115, *Landing Ship, Tank (LST) 1942–2002*

4

the LCI's hull was the Landing Craft, Support (Large) Mk 3, the LCS(L)(3). The LCS(L) was variously known as the "Whoofus" and "Mighty Midget." These were all specialized fire support craft intended to place suppressive fire on landing beaches using guns, automatic cannons, rockets, and mortars. The principal conversions discussed in this book are:

Landing Craft, Infantry (Gun)	LCI(G)
Landing Craft, Infantry (Mortar)	LCI(M)
Landing Craft, Infantry (Rocket)	LCI(R)
Landing Ship, Medium (Rocket)	LSM(R)
Landing Craft, Support (Large) Mk 3	LCS(L)(3)
Landing Craft (Flotilla Flagship)	LC(FF)

LCS(L)(3)-3 clad in a navy green and pale green camouflage scheme. All LCSs were fitted with radar for surface search, air warning, and also positioning in order to fire their rockets accurately.

LANDING CRAFT, INFANTRY – DEVELOPMENT

In late 1941 and early 1942, development was underway for two large beaching vessels vastly different in size and capabilities, but designed as companion amphibious vessels. The LST and Landing Craft, Tank (LCT) were both based on British requirements and versions were built on both sides of the Atlantic. The LST was a big ship, almost 330ft in length and capable of carrying 20 medium tanks, while the 114ft LCT possessed a bow ramp and an open cargo compartment capable of carrying five medium tanks. LST vessels were capable of trans-oceanic movement, but the LCT was not so seaworthy and one of the LST's many roles was to transport LCTs overseas either as deck cargo or disassembled and carried in the copious tank deck.

The British had another requirement, what they initially referred to as a "giant raiding craft" (GRC). To keep the Germans in occupied Europe off balance, and to conduct some form of offensive operations, the British were executing minor coastal raids. Small landing craft were used in this role, such as the Landing Craft, Assault (LCA), a 41ft boat carrying 35 troops. These lacked the capacity for transporting more than just small detachments, and their endurance, speed, range, and cross-Channel capabilities were poor. What was desired was a 150ft beaching vessel

The pilothouse of LSM-34 was similar in design to that on LCI(L)-31 class boats, with "castle bridges" but taller, the height necessary in order to provide vision over the high forecastle and elevated bow ramp. The canvas awning over the conn was removed in combat zones to provide full overhead observation to detect aircraft.

LCI(L)-412 under construction at the George Lawley & Sons Shipbuilding Corp., Neponset, MA, in January 1944. The LCI's box-like hull design can readily be seen.

The stern of LCI(L)-443 provides a view of the large foot-like skegs protecting the props forward of the rudders. The kedge anchor and rack are on the transom and the engine exhaust and coolant water ports, emitting spray, can be seen on the side just above the waterline. To the right of the three stacked fog oil drums is the Besler smoke generator.

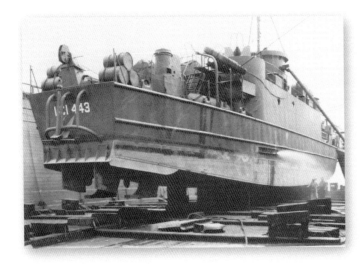

capably of carrying 200 troops – a rifle company – at 20 knots with a range of 230 miles. The low-silhouetted vessel needed adequate air defense features and protection from small arms fire, as it was expected to discharge its raiders directly ashore and not have to wait offshore and carry smaller landing craft to deliver and retrieve the troops. It would also provide accommodation for troops for up to two days. Looking into the future, it was realized that such a vessel would be valuable for the planned invasion of the Continent.

As an interim measure, the British had converted cross-Channel ferries, minesweepers, and other vessels into Landing Ships, Infantry, Medium and Small – LSI(M) and LSI(S). These vessels were almost 400ft long and carried between 200 and 400 troops, depending on the particular ship. They typically carried eight LCAs or similar landing craft – they were not beaching vessels.

By the time the development of what would become the LCI was underway, the British had begun to conduct fewer coastal raids as the Germans strengthened the Atlantic Wall. Development continued, though, as the LCI would be an ideal craft to deliver follow-on infantry during the projected summer 1943 invasion of France. It was not conceived as an initial-wave assault craft. The British commission hoping to find a builder in America discovered that private builders such as Higgins were not only fully committed to contracts, but were running behind. British building capacity was unable to handle any additional projects. The US Navy was none too interested in such a raiding craft and had little faith in larger landing craft, feeling they were too vulnerable to air attack. As with the LST, the British approached the US Army. In order for the US to construct Lend-Lease ships for the British, the design also had to be intended for use by the US armed forces. The US Army was indeed interested in the LCI, realizing the need to land larger follow-on units than was feasible by Landing Craft, Personnel (LCP) or Landing Craft, Vehicle (LCV) carrying a platoon-minus.

The British needed 300 craft by April 1943, a year away, and the design was little more than a sketch. There were no shipping capabilities for vessels this size, so it had to be capable of trans-oceanic crossings. It needed a 500nm (575-mile) endurance and required a speed of at least 15 knots, 20 preferred. To save space and weight, and speed up production, a bow ramp and doors were forfeited. Instead the troops would disembark using three or four 2ft 6in-wide gangway ramps from weather-deck level. There was no capability to deliver even light vehicles, wheeled crew-served weapons such as antitank guns, or bulk cargo. BuShips revised the design in May. It was hoped to be capable of better than 15 knots, beach on a 1:50 ratio gradient, and provide limited small arms fire protection. Armament would be four 20mm guns. Early proposals foresaw it being unarmed when carrying troops, instead relying on the passengers' armaments, with 20mm guns mounted when no troops were embarked, to prevent overloading. This set-up, of course, was impractical as once the troops debarked the vessel, in the forefront of the action, the vessel was unable to protect itself from aircraft attacking the beachhead and shipping.

The final design emerged as 160ft long with a 23ft beam, and had a forward beaching draft of 2ft 6in and 4ft 5in at the stern. It could carry three weeks' stores for a crew of three officers and 21 enlisted men and six troop officers and 182 enlisted men. Instead of troops it could also carry 75 tons of cargo, but only in containers that a single stevedore could carry. It would be propelled by eight General Motors engines, four per shaft. The design was kept simple, with as few curves as possible to speed up production. The result was a boxy-looking craft with a blunt bow, flat bottom, and a low rectangular deckhouse with an unhandsome "square bridge" forward of the deckhouse. This design was initially called the Troop Transport (Short-Radius) (APY). Production began in July 1942 and the design was soon redesignated the Landing Craft, Infantry (Large) – LCI(L). In this book the "(L)" is not always included and does not refer to a different craft.

LCI(L) CONSTRUCTION

The first APY contract was signed on June 3, 1942. The first contracted yards were George Lawley & Sons Shipbuilding Corp., Neponset, MA, and New York Shipbuilding Corp., Camden, NJ. New Jersey Shipbuilding Corp., Barber, NJ, would be the most prolific of the ten builders. Two prototype LCI(L)s were launched, LCI-1 and LCI-209 (the latter actually the first to be completed), and were tested in September and October 1942, respectively. It was found that they could beach and retract very well, but they could not maneuver in reverse. One boat had been built without prop skegs, the guards protecting the propellers, and turned in a 75yd radius. The boat with skegs required a 100yd radius. Regardless, since the props were so vulnerable to beaching damage it was directed that all boats have skegs. Trans-Atlantic crossing was critical, and eight LCIs accompanied by three tugs sailed from Norfolk, VA, to Bermuda in late 1942. They weathered Force 4 winds (13–18mph) and 8ft seas, proving they were capable of such a passage in moderate weather. The boats made 11 knots, but rolled and yawed badly, and heavy bow-on waves actually rippled the hull plates. A redesign increased the displacement, however, so that they drew some 6ft of water when fully loaded for ocean transit, with a speed just shy of 14 knots in fair weather. They were too slow to accompany attack transport groups and had to depart port ahead of the faster ships along with the LSTs.

LCI(L)-351, the lead ship of the 351 class, was commissioned in May 1943. It was converted to an LCI(G) in December 1944 and to an LCI(M) in April 1945. The boat was struck from the Naval Register in 1946 and sold for scrap in 1948. Such was the typical life of an LCI.

The 299 LCI(L)-1 class boats (1–48, 61–136, 161–196, 209–350) were built largely according to British plans owing to Britain's urgent need. Various changes were made to the original British design to accommodate American construction methods. Other changes eliminated the bench-type main deck troop seats (behind the bulwark and alongside the deckhouse), changed the bicycle (x12) stowage compartment to general storage, and added a level to the bridge to provide the conn with better vision over the bow.

Construction time varied and improved with experience, but on average construction took 5–6 weeks from laying down the keel to launching and about another 5–6 weeks for fitting before the vessel was commissioned. The craft were constructed in sections, essentially end-to-end boxes, which were simply welded together on the slip. At the height of construction, in some yards a new LCI was sliding down the ways at the rate of one every day or two.

Although the LCI was considered a follow-on landing craft, it was still provided with some armor. This was 15lb per square foot special treatment steel (STS) protecting the bridge and conn. The forward third of the hull sides and the bulwark forward of the deckhouse were 10lb STS. The bulwark, two parallel low steel walls on the forward weather deck, protected troops preparing to debark as well as the egress hatches from the troop compartments. The bridge, conn, and gun tubs were additionally protected by 2¾in plastic armor.

Lessons were learned and flaws were uncovered in the LCI-1 class and it was not long before a redesign was underway. Forty-five LCI-1s were canceled so that an improved design could be built sooner. The deckhouse of the new LCI-351 class was extended forward and widened to the hull sides. The egress hatches from troop compartments No. 2–4 were now enclosed by the deckhouse, reducing problems troops had coming topside in foul weather; only No. 3 was so protected on the LCI-1 class. The hatches were enlarged to accept litters. Previously there was deck space on either side of the deckhouse allowing free passage. Now one had to pass through the deckhouse when moving fore and aft. The enlarged deckhouse provided more messing, troop officer accommodation, and crew work areas necessary for the voyages, which were longer than originally envisioned. Galley space, refrigeration units and the numbers of toilets and washrooms were also

 LCI(L)-1 CLASS AND LCI(L)-351 CLASS

1: LCI(L)-1 CLASS This early production boat retains the seldom-used steadying sail mast on the aft end of the deckhouse. These masts were later removed. It also features the "park bench" seats along the port inboard side of the bulwark, but similar seats on the outside of the bulkheads of the deckhouse were deleted. The early boats were armed with four 20mm guns. This boat is painted haze gray, but once in the Pacific was repainted in a green camouflage scheme. Gray was often retained in the Mediterranean and the English Channel. Small white hull numbers were used to limit the vessels' visibility. It was soon found that larger numbers were necessary for control purposes and this necessity overruled low visibility.

2: LCI(L)-351 CLASS The much redesigned and improved 351 class offered accommodations for lengthier cruises and added a fifth 20mm gun. The hull did not change, but the deckhouse was enlarged and there was some internal compartment redesign. The Pacific dapple camouflage scheme was designed to blend into the vegetated shoreline of islands in the background (from water level). This scheme was especially effective in the Solomons, with its many closely gathered islands. In daylight the vessels would moor at the shore's edge to blend into the trees. The round "castle bridge" is apparent as opposed to the "square bridge" on the earlier class.

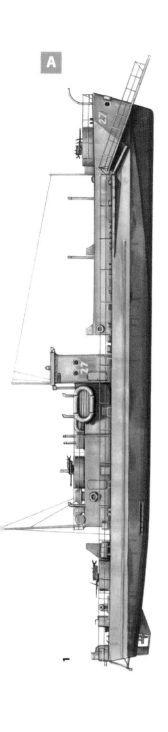

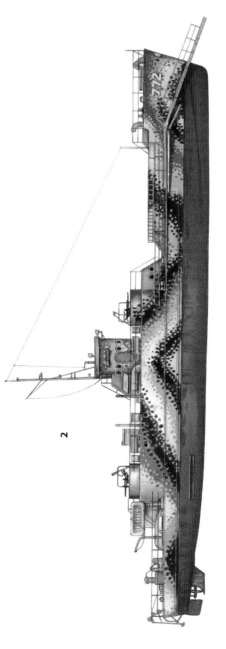

A

1

2

increased. Improved heating and ventilation were provided and bunks installed in the troop compartments. Power connections were fitted to allow crew and passengers to remain aboard when docked. Underway refueling facilities were also installed. The new class could carry nine troop officers and 206 enlisted men and had a crew of four officers and 25 men. A taller round "castle bridge" replaced the "square bridge" and four 20mm guns were mounted on the deckhouse's corners. A fifth gun was on the bow. The two gangway ramps were lengthened by 4ft to provide a more gradual incline and were now lowered and retracted by the anchor windlass rather than by hand-run block-and-tackle. The first LCI(L)-351 class was laid down on March 5, 1943, launched on April 8, and commissioned on May 14. This lead ship and others would be converted to gunboats and then mortar boats. A total of 595 LCI(L)-351 class were built: 351–716, 731–780, 784–821, 866–884, 943–1033, and 1052–1098 (inclusive of the LCI-402 subclass).

Many of the users called for a centerline bow ramp and doors similar to those on an LST. Such features would allow troops to debark faster and at beach level rather than being exposed while descending the narrow ramps. Bulkier cargo could also be offloaded faster by hand. The prototype was LCI(L)-402. Bow doors were installed on craft built after June 1, 1944, to include: 402, 641–657, 691–716, 762–780, 782–821, 866–884, 1024–1033, and 1068–1098. Other changes to this subclass were minor.

A total of 211 LCI(L)s were transferred to the Royal Navy under Lend-Lease from 1943, with the crews trained in the States. In early 1945, 25 more were transferred to the USSR, with the crews trained by Coast Guardsmen at Cold Bay, Alaska. No fire support types were transferred to either navy.

Armament

LCIs were provided with only light anti-aircraft armament, four or five 20mm guns. Later versions substituted a 40mm for the bow 20mm. The various fire support craft had a much varied armament, with combinations of 20mm and 40mm cannons, 3in or 5in guns, 4.2in mortars, and 4.5in or 5in barrage rockets.

The Oerlikon 20mm Mk 4 automatic cannon was the standard armament of LCIs and LSMs. Fed by 60-round snail drum magazines, it rattled out shells at 550rpm with a 2,000yd range and was manned by a crew of five. Mk 24 twin mounts were fitted on later LSM(R)s and added two men. Numbers of .50cal M2 Browning air-cooled machine guns were mounted on LCI gunboats and LSM(R)s, mostly on the fantail, as were Browning .30cal M1919A4 machine guns on LSM(R)s. These served as last-resort weapons against air attack, but were also useful against small attack boats. The British usually mounted two .303in Lewis Mk I machine guns for air defense on their LCI(L)s.

Heavier anti-aircraft weapons were provided in the form of 40mm Bofors guns on the gunboats. These were also used against targets ashore. The dual Mk 1 mount was usually on the stern and/or bow and consisted of a Mk 1 right gun and Mk 2 left gun. These were US Navy weapons employing powered mounts and were water-cooled, making them capable of a high sustained rate of fire. The single-barrel 40mm Mk 3 gun was a US Army M1 on a US Navy Mk 3 mount; often Army M1 mounts were simply welded to the deck in the rush to convert LCIs to gunboats, plus the mount was smaller and lighter. These were air-cooled and manually trained. Single and dual guns had four- and seven-man crews, respectively. The "forty-mike-mike" was fed by four-round clips and fired at 120–180rpm to 5,000yd.

The LSM(R) boasted the heaviest armament in the form of the 5in (38cal) Mk 12 gun in a fully enclosed Mk 30 turret, as used on destroyers. This gun threw a 55lb shell to a range of 17,000yd. The 12-man crew, using ready rounds in the turret, could hammer out 25rpm. With a steady supply of ammunition from the magazine, they could maintain 15rpm. While the vessel's rocket armament (see below) saturated the target area, the 5in was an accurate and potent weapon against point targets with high-explosive (called "common" by the Navy), anti-aircraft, armor-piercing, and illumination (called "star" by the Navy) shells.

A little-used weapon found on some gunboats and LCS(R)s was the 3in (50cal) Mk 22 dual-purpose gun. This was often mounted in lieu of a twin 40mm. The outdated Mk 22 was moderately effective against aircraft but too light for surface targets, and the high rate of 40mm fire was much preferred over the 3in's 18rpm. It had a 14,000yd range, was manned by seven men, and used the same type of ammunition as the 5in gun.

LCI(M)s and LSM(R)s also mounted four US Army 4.2in M2 mortars. These weapons, relatively small compared to other naval armament, had a 600–3,200yd range – further than the 4.5in rocket – but they could not be fired to their full 4,400yd range because of the stress inflicted on the deck. While the barrage-launch of 480 rockets was an impressive display, reload time was considerable and demanding on manpower. A 4.2in mortar could fire 40 rounds in the first two minutes and 100 rounds in the first 20 minutes. The four mortars together could each keep up a steady barrage of 60 rounds an hour indefinitely. Ammunition included high-explosive, white phosphorus, and illumination.

Three types of barrage rockets were launched from fire support craft. These rockets were developed and fielded in a remarkably short time. The

The 20mm Mk 4 cannon atop the deck of an LCI(L)-1 class boat. The odd pipe arrangement to the gun tub's left is the folded stovepipe. The gun is mounted over the galley.

4.5in "Old Faithful" beach barrage rocket was quickly designed using the motor of the 2.25in Mousetrap anti-submarine rocket fitted with a 20lb general-purpose bomb. It was first fired in late June and thousands were launched during the North Africa invasion in November 1942, but from LCTs, not LCIs. The 4.5in rocket was fin-stabilized with only a 1,100yd range, and was none too accurate. Both high-explosive and white phosphorus warheads were provided. A slightly longer-ranged model with a longer rocket motor was provided in 1944. The barrage rockets (BR) were fired from several types of launcher racks:

Mk 1 – 12 rockets in four layers, elevatable, but non-trainable.[2]
Mk 7 – 12-rocket gravity-fed racks. Preset elevations, but non-trainable. Fired 12 rockets in four seconds.
Mk 8 – 12 rockets, modified Mk 1 with fixed elevation, non-trainable.
Mk 11 – Improved Mk 7 capable of jettisoning misfires.
Mk 22 – 12 rockets. Elevatable, fixed train.

Five-inch forward-firing aircraft rockets aboard an early LCI(R). These are four-round fixed-elevation Mk 36 racks. On the sides, trained outboard for loading, are six-round elevatable Mk 30 racks; three rockets were fitted above and three below each launcher arm. They would be trained ahead for firing.

Because of the inadequate range and accuracy of the 4.5in, development of a new rocket began in May 1943. The 5in high-velocity spinner rocket (HVSR)[3] began to be fitted on rocket boats in late 1944. Two motor variants were available offering 5,000yd and 10,000yd ranges with various high-explosive, semi-armor-piercing, and white phosphorus warheads. The Mk 51 was a single rail launcher similar to the Mk 7 capable of automatically firing 12 rockets in 4.5 seconds. The Mk 102 was a trainable, automatically loaded (from below deck) twin-tube launcher capable of firing 30 rockets per minute.

As an interim measure owing the non-availability of the new 5in HVSR, the first LSM(R)s were fitted with racks for the much longer fin-stabilized 5in forward-firing aircraft rocket (FFAC). Fitted with high-explosive and white phosphorus warheads, it had only a 1,700yd range. The late-war launchers required long rails: the Mk 30 had six rails and the Mk 36 four. Both were fixed in train, but the Mk 30 was elevatable while the Mk 36 was fixed at 45 degrees.

A Type C rack for a single 300lb Mk 6 depth charge was fitted on either side of the fantail on the LCI(L)-1 class, the idea being that the LCIs could

---

[2] Mk 1 Mod 0 was port, Mk 1 Mod 1 was starboard.
[3] These are often identified as "SS" rockets, which means "spin-stabilized," but are sometimes misidentified as "ship-to-shore."

B **LCI(L)-402 CLASS AND LCS(L)(3)**

1: LCI(L)-402 CLASS From June 1944, LCIs began to be built with a bow ramp and doors and a redesigned forecastle. Some vessels of this LCI(L)-402 class were converted to LCI(R)s, with rocket launchers on the forward deck and a 40mm gun on the forecastle, and LC(FF)s. The pale blue upper hull and deckhouse and navy blue lower hull scheme were often used in the English Channel.

2: LCS(L)(3) While the hull was the same, with some modification of the bow, and the "castle bridge" was used, the LCS(L) bore little resemblance to the LCI(L) on which it was based. Ten rocket launchers were fitted just forward of the deckhouse and No. 2 gun tube, but it was foremost a gunboat, with twin 40mms forward of the pilothouse and on the fantail. The bow featured a 3in or single 40mm gun, or a twin 40mm. A common camouflage scheme was for the hull to be painted black from the stern to a point at the forward gun and angled to appear as a vessel's bow. The forward position of the hull, deckhouse, gun tubes, other fittings, and the bulwark from the No. 2 gun mount (3in gun in this case) forward to the bow were haze gray. Some vessels had a broad black waterline band and red hull bottom.

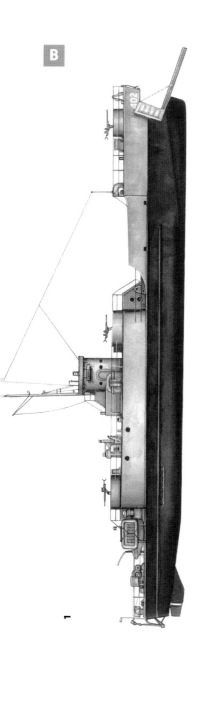

1

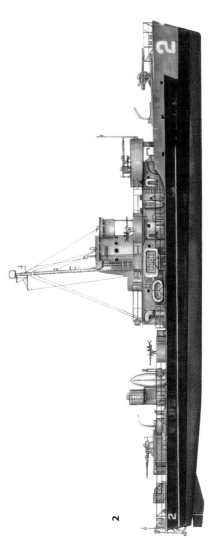

2

B

LCI(L) characteristics		
	LCI(L)-1 class	**LCI(L)-351 class**
Dimensions		
Length:	158ft 5½in	160ft 4in
Beam:	23ft 3in	23ft 3in
Displacement		
Loaded:	387 tons	385 tons
Landing:	238 tons	257½ tons
Light:	194 tons	209 tons
Draft		
Loaded:	5ft 4in forward, 5ft 11in aft	5ft 8in forward & aft
Landing:	2ft 8in forward, 5ft aft	2ft 10in forward, 5ft 3in aft
Light:	3ft 3in mean	3ft 6in mean
Speed		
Maximum:	15½ knots	15½ knots
Endurance		
12 knots:	8,700 miles	8,000 miles

help protect convoys from submarines. These were often later removed and were not installed on the LCI(L)-351 class. Most LCIs had a Besler fog oil smoke generator on the fantail and were also provided with M3 or Mk 2 smoke pots, which could be burned in onboard racks, or M4A2 floating pots dropped over the side.

LCI(L) DESCRIPTION

The LCI(L) was the third-largest of the beaching craft, being outsized by the LST and LSM. While not intended as an assault craft, it was a combatant built to beach itself on a hostile shore where it could be under artillery, mortar, and small arms fire as well as exposed to air attack. In the fire support role, while operating offshore, it was also exposed to and drew heavy fire.

From the keel up, an LCI had four or five levels. The hold was divided into dozens of compartments including ballast tanks, fuel oil tanks, fresh water tanks, and voids. The LCI(L)-1 class held 120 tons of fuel, 240gal of lubricating oil, and 36 tons of fresh water, while the LCI(L)-351 class carried 10 tons less fuel and one ton more water. The first platform contained four troop compartments, engine room, crew quarters, storage, and steering gear. The main or weather deck forward of the deckhouse contained only the bulwark sheltering troops on deck. Forward was the forecastle (fo'c's'le – pronounced "folk'-s'l"), a raised platform mounting a 20mm gun and flanked by the gangway ramps. Aft of the deckhouse was the fantail. The deckhouse was divided into numerous compartments to accommodate the crew, passengers, and vessel operations. The bridge was at the deckhouse's forward end and included the raised conn. One or four guns, depending on the class, were atop the deckhouse.

Propulsion

The engine room was below the aft end of the deckhouse. Propulsion was provided by eight General Motors Detroit 6-71 two-stroke, six-cylinder, 225hp diesel engines. These collectively developed 1,800hp. Most ships had one large engine per shaft, but a suitably sized and powered engine did not exist for the LCI. It would have required far too long to develop such an engine and engine factories were already overloaded. An ingenious solution was found by linking four engines together to power each shaft. The GM 6-71 was a tried and proven design used for buses, trucks, tanks, tugboats, and generators. Normally, linking four engines to a common reduction gear would develop harmonic oscillations capable of breaking crankshafts. This problem was overcome by using dry disc clutches with just enough plate tension to allow the clutch to slip when abnormal vibrations occurred. The oscillations would then go out of phase with one another. Individual engines could be taken offline

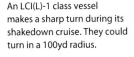

An LCI(L)-1 class vessel makes a sharp turn during its shakedown cruise. They could turn in a 100yd radius.

while underway (with a slight speed reduction) for servicing. There were instances when LCIs limped into port on one to three engines that were kept running on parts cannibalized from the others.

Each engine had an exhaust line with a small port just above the waterline, four on each side. Seawater both cooled the engines' heat exchangers and quietened the wet-type Maxim silencers. Hot coolant water and exhaust fumes were discharged through the same exhaust ports. This system enabled an LCI to approach a hostile shore in comparative silence. Two GM 2-71 two-cylinder versions of the main engines powered the two 20kW power generators for the 120-volt DC electrical system. There were dozens of small electric motors to operate water, fuel, and bilge pumps, fire fighting systems, etc.

The engines were not capable of running in reverse, which was of course essential for docking maneuvers and extracting from a beach. Two bronze 4ft-diameter variable-pitch propellers were provided for this purpose. They were always turning in the same direction, but when reverse was required an electric servo motor, located between the forward two engines, reversed the angle of the three blades to the astern pitch. The propellers turned constantly, even when the ship came to a rest, when the blades were pitched to the feathering position where they imparted no movement. The pitch motor operated from 24-volt batteries in the event that both power generators were lost. Two additional electric motors powered the steering, which was performed by two rudders. If the power generators were lost, there was a manual steering station on the fantail. A sound-powered telephone provided steering instructions from the conn to the wheel station, which was blind forward.

LCI(L)s and LCS(L)s were powered by eight of these reliable General Motors Detroit 6-71 two-stroke, six-cylinder, 225hp diesel engines, four per propeller shaft.

Below decks

In the narrow bow beneath the forecastle were voids and stores compartments. The layout was similar on both the LCI(L)-1 and 351 classes. Troop compartment capacity for each compartment is parenthesized, the first number for the LCI(L)-1 class, second for the 351 class, and the third for the 402 class: troop compartment No. 1 (46/48/47); No. 2 (58/62/62); and No. 3 (67/67/63). Doghouse hatches to the main deck for No. 1 and 2 were within the forward bulwark, while No. 3 exited into the deckhouse on the LCI(L)-1. On the LCI(L)-351 both No. 2 and 3 gave access into the deckhouse. The crew quarters accommodating all enlisted men was aft of troop compartment No. 3 and forward of the engine room, while the engine room was below the aft end of the deckhouse and also housed the power generators. No. 4 troop compartment (28/23/26) was aft of the engine room with a ladder leading to a companionway nnected to the deckhouse on the 351 and 402 classes. On the LCI(L)-1 class it was protected only by a doghouse hatch on the fantail. Two provisions compartments were to the aft of the No. 4 troop compartment with a companionway separating them and connecting the troop compartment and the steering gear compartment in the lazarette (aft-most compartment).

LCI(L)-419 beached on Utah Beach, Normandy. Engine coolant intakes were on the hull bottom on most ships, but since the LCI was by nature frequently run aground, they were on the sides where they would not suck up sand. In the English Channel, US vessels bore a large "US" while British vessels lacked identifying letters.

C ANATOMY OF AN LCI(L)-351 CLASS

The LCI(L) consisted of three levels. The "first platform" contained various storage spaces, four troop compartments, crew quarters, and engine room. Beneath this was the "hold," divided into many small compartments for ballast, fuel, water and serving as voids. The "main deck" included the forward deck with the bulwark and the fantail aft of the deckhouse. The "deckhouse" contained a surprising number of compartments and facilities to serve the crew and passengers and operate the vessel. The "forecastle and deckhouse" topside mounted the armament and the pilothouse.

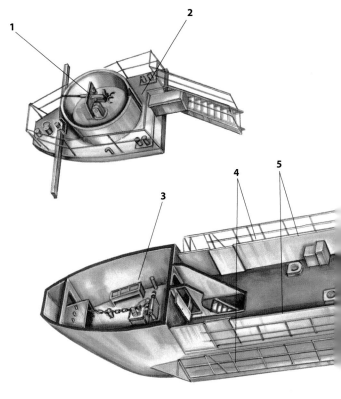

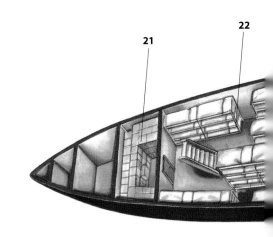

KEY

1 20mm Mk 4 automatic cannon (x5)
2 Forecastle
3 Anchor room, troops' head
4 Troop gangway ramps
5 Bulwarks
6 Pilot house
7 Conn
8 Troops officers' quarters
9 Enlisted mess
10 Ship's officers' quarters
11 Officers' mess
12 Ward room
13 Galley
14 Refrigerators
15 Life rafts
16 Chart & radio room
17 Captain's quarters
18 Officers' head
19 Crew's head
20 Stern anchor winch
21 Stores
22 No. 1 troop compartment
23 No. 2 troop compartment
24 No. 3 troop compartment
25 Crews' quarters
26 Engine room
27 General Motors Detroit 6-71, 225hp diesel engines (x8)
28 No. 4 troop compartment
29 Magazines & stores
30 Lazarette & steering gear

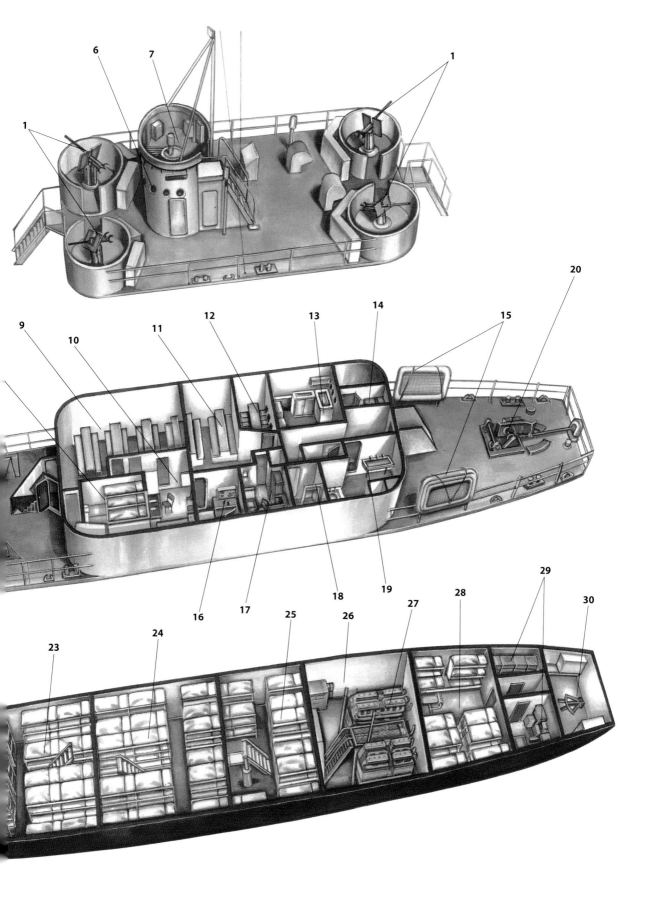

The troop and crew compartments were crowded with quadruple-stacked bunks with very narrow spaces between them. There were no lockers for troops (they lived out of their backpacks) and only limited lockers for crewmen. Lighting and ventilation were poor, but were improved somewhat in the 351 class.

Main deck

The main forward deck between the forecastle and the deckhouse held the bulwark. This was simply two low bulkheads inset from the hull sides and running from the forecastle almost back to the deckhouse. It provided a degree of small arms fire and fragmentation protection to troops coming on deck. Doghouse and emergency trunk hatches were behind the bulwark. To gain access to the ramps, the troops could go around the aft end of the bulwark or through a steel side gate on each side. The fantails of the LCI(L)-1 and 351 classes were much different. Both had large power winches to retract the stern anchor and the kedge anchor was mounted on a rack on the stern. The 1 class had two 20mm gun tubs on the fantail, the port side gun being slightly more aft than the starboard, and there was a single depth charge rack on either side. Troop compartment No. 4 doghouse hatch was just forward of the port gun. Two life rafts and a 12ft skiff were stowed here on the 351 class. On the 1 class its two rafts were stowed on either side of the deckhouse. The rafts were only sufficient for the crew, the passengers having to rely on life jackets.

Deckhouse

The major difference between the 1 class and 351 class was the deckhouse. The 1 class had a comparatively small rectangular deckhouse with the bridge forward. Often called the "square bridge," it was actually trapezoid in shape with a radio mast positioned abaft. The antenna wire ran forward to a short mast abaft the forecastle gun. The lower portion of the bridge was the

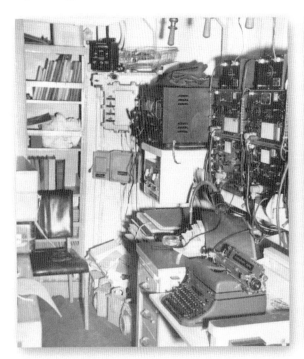
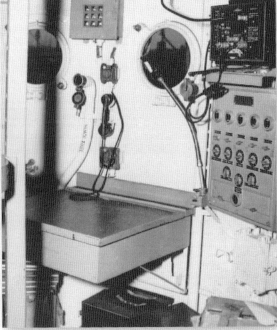

pilothouse and the upper the conn. On most boats in American service, the conn was elevated another level to provide better vision forward. The deckhouse proper held crew and passenger officer quarters, wardroom, radio room, galley, head, and washroom. The 1 class was designed only for a 48-hour transit with troops, and mess and sanitation facilities were barely adequate. A 20mm tub was abaft the conn along with ventilators. There were hatches on both sides of the bridge and the aftward sides of the deckhouse. Two portholes pierced the sides and front of the bridge. The conn was open-topped. Originally a tall mast was fitted abaft the deckhouse, intended to rig a triangular steadying sail. This was to reduce rolling in rough seas, but did little to steady the ship, and was usually removed.

The 351 class deckhouse was considerably larger in length and breadth. It extended further forward and aft and occupied the full width of the deck. Rather than being rectangular, its corners were rounded with a 20mm tub on each. The most notable feature was the high round bridge called a "castle bridge" set one-third of the way back atop the deckhouse. There was a hatch on both sides, with ports all round, and a ladder to the aft for access to the conn, beside which was a radio and signal mast. Ladders on the forward and aft ends of the deckhouse accessed its topside. A central passageway ran the length of the deckhouse. On the starboard side was a mess, small wardroom, galley, and refrigerator rooms. On the port side were troop and ship's officer quarters, chart and radio room, captain's cabin, officer's head and washroom, and crew head and washroom.

Forecastle and ramps

The raised forecastle platform housed toilets and a washroom for the troops plus the bow anchor winch. More facilities were added to the 351 class, which also had a slightly raised overhead platform. Atop the forecastle was a 20mm tub and a spare anchor was stowed there. The main anchor was housed on the forepeak. A very few 351 class lacked the bow 20mm. A 2ft 6in-wide ramp was fitted on either side of the forecastle, 28ft long for the 1 class and 32ft for the 351 class. Stanchions with cable handrails were fitted on both sides of the ramps. Retractable catheads (arms supporting block-and-tackle) were fitted to the forepeak to support the tackle lowering and raising the ramps. They were lowered by hand on the 1 class and by the anchor winch on the 351 class.

ABOVE LEFT
Details of an LCI's 2ft 6in-wide troop ramp. On the LCI(L)-1 class it was 28ft long and 32ft on the LCI(L)-351 class. The longer ramp provided a less steep incline for equipment-laden troops. Cable handrails and tread slats aided the troops on a wet ramp. The I-beam cathead supporting the ramp's block-and-tackle was pivoted inboard when not in use.

ABOVE RIGHT
Here we can see the design differences between the LCI(L)-351 class with two troop ramps (right) and the LCI(L) 402-subclass with bow doors and a 4ft 6in-wide single ramp (left).

Some boats had alternate debarkation ladders stowed on the outboard bulwark sides. These were placed almost vertically on either side of the forepeak forward of the ramp catheads. The ramps, what the British called "brows," were sometimes torn off by heavy surf or fouled in wreckage. The 402 class, with an internal bow ramp, had a much rearranged forecastle. The single centerline gangway ramp angled downward to the drop ramp. The ramp was accessed from the weather deck and not the forward troop compartment. A wide double hatch was provided in the forecastle's aft bulkhead to access the ramp. The bow ramp only extended 4ft and was 4ft 6in wide. A 20ft extension ramp of the same width could be slid out to reach 16ft beyond the ramp's end. The bow doors were secured by turnbuckle dogs. Doors and ramp were operated by cables via a heavy winch fitted in the center of the main deck. The bulwarks were moved outboard to the side of the hull to provide more unrestricted deck cargo space. The interior of the forecastle now served as storage with the head and washroom in the deckhouse.

The closed bow doors of LCI(L)-402. This craft is painted haze gray, as were most LCIs destined for the Mediterranean and Europe. Those for the Pacific were usually colored green in the yard and sometimes even painted in a camouflage scheme. This also provides details of the bow anchor.

LCI VARIANTS

To serve as command ships for landing craft flotillas, 49 LCIs were converted in late 1944 to Landing Craft (Flotilla Flagship) – LC(FF). These served as flotilla leaders not only for LCI units, but LSM and LST units also. (It was impractical to convert these larger landing ships to command ships due to the loss of cargo capacity.) Externally the LC(FF) appeared no different than a standard LCI other than having a small radar dome atop the mast and a long whip antenna aft of the pilothouse. The troop compartments were converted to accommodate the increased complement, with No. 1 compartment becoming the enlisted staff quarters, No. 2 the staff workspace, No. 3 being divided into two-man cabins for up to eight staff officers,[4] and No. 4 serving as

4 Flotilla staff officers included communications and engineering officers, paymaster, and doctor.

 LCI FIRE SUPPORT CRAFT

The various fire support craft based on the LCI(L) were converted from LCI(L)-1 class, LCI(L)-351 class, and even the LCI(L)-402 class with a bow door and ramp. As well as being converted while under construction in US yards, they were also converted overseas in advance naval bases. Armament configurations varied between craft of the same type, sometimes drastically.

1: LCI(G)-397 was converted to a Type B gunboat in June 1943. Besides the early Pacific theater gunboat conversions, those converted in the United States had one of six battery configurations. The types A, B, and E were built on LCI(L)-351 and 402 class vessels and the Types C, D, and F on the LCI(L)-1 class. Only the 20mm, 40mm, and 3in guns are depicted on the plan diagrams for the LCI(G)-351 class gunboats. The rocket launchers were mounted in place of the troop ramps. Full armament is described in the text.

2: LCI(R)-73 was a 1 class boat outfitted with 12 x 4.5in Mk 1 rocket launchers.

3: LCI(M)-265 mounted a 40mm on the bow, 4 x 20mm in the usual LCI(L)-351 class manner on the deckhouse, and three 4.2in mortars, one on the centerline between the bulwarks and two immediately forward, either side of the deckhouse.

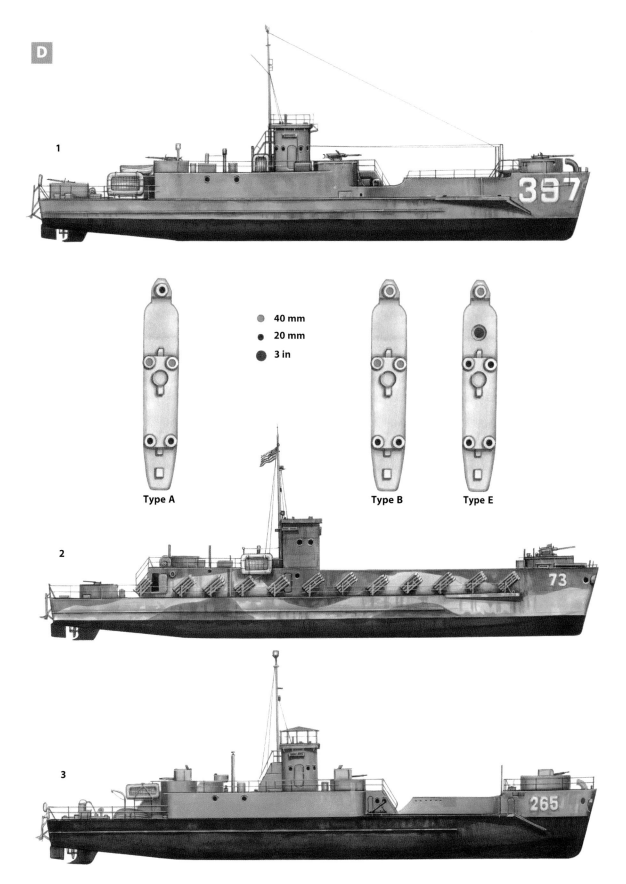

D

1

● 40 mm
● 20 mm
● 3 in

Type A   Type B   Type E

2

3

21

The forecastle of LCI(G)-561 with its 40mm Mk 3 and two 20mm Mk 4 anti-aircraft guns. To the right can be seen 4.5in Mk 7 rocket racks. The light-colored (gray) rectangular containers in front of the 40mm are ammunition cans. Its ready ammunition box is open to the right. Beneath the 20mm platform wooden ammunition crates are visible.

provisions storage. The former troop officers' quarters was converted into the flotilla commander's cabin. There were two 30kW generators instead of 20kW and a water evaporator was installed as well as additional radios. Besides command, operational planning, and coordination, the flotilla relied on the LC(FF) to guide the other craft to their destination. Some of these craft were in action at Okinawa and proved to be too slow and small to provide the necessary accommodations and workspace and they were retired at the war's end. Conversions to LC(FF) were: 367–370, 399, 423–427, 484–486, 503, 504, 531-533, 535, 536, 569, 571, 572, 575, 627, 628, 656, 657, 679, 775, 782, 783, 788–793, 988, 994, 995, 998, 1031, and 1079–1083.

Earlier some LCIs were converted locally to flagships in the Mediterranean and known unofficially as LCI(H) – Headquarters. These were also used at Normandy and in late 1944 additional communications capabilities were added to 11 LCIs as LCI(L)(C)s – Command – to support the southern France landing.

There were two other unofficial conversions, produced with only minor internal modifications made in-theater. The LCI(A)s – Ammunition – were standard LCIs with the No. 2 troop compartment bunks removed to store 1,200 rounds of 4.2in mortar ammunition. These craft supported LCI(M)s, with an enlarged crew to pass ammunition. The LCI(D)s – Diver – transported and served as mother ships for 100-man underwater demolition teams (UDTs). The LCI(D) vessels were numbered 29, 44, 227, and 448.

When the concept of the fire support craft was developed, the LCI(L) was considered ideal for conversion. It was large enough to mount substantial armament, had sufficient space for ammunition and a larger crew, could operate in shallow inshore waters, was capable of seagoing operations (thus allowing it to self-deploy to objective islands), and conversion was at a relatively low cost. In addition, there was a surplus of LCIs being built, so conversion would not limit the availability of dedicated troop-carrying LCIs. The gun-, rocket-, and mortar-armed craft were of similar layout, but with different mixes of armament. They were not armed purely with the stated armament: mortar and rocket boats had guns and most of the gunboats also had rockets. The internal compartment arrangement was changed, with No. 1 forward troop compartment becoming a stores compartment, No. 2 troop compartment converted to a magazine, the amidships troop compartment now being for the additional crew, and the aft troop compartment serving as another magazine. The superstructure changed little (both square and round bridge classes were used), except for the addition of fire-control systems. The troop ramps were usually removed, as often were the bulwarks. Armament arrangement varied greatly, even between craft of the same type.

Landing Craft, Infantry (Gun)

The LCI(G) gunboats were converted in the largest numbers from 1 class and 351 class boats, 86 in total, and had the largest crews: five officers and 65 men. LCI(G)-22, 24, 68, and 69 were converted at New Caledonia in August 1943, mounting 1x 3in, 1 x 40mm aft, 4 x 20mm, and 6 x .50cal

The crew loads 4.5in barrage rockets into 12-round Mk 7 racks aboard a Type D LCI(G) gunboat, Peleliu, September 1944. The pipe framework aft of the bow 40mm prevents the gun from being fired into the deckhouse when tracking aircraft.

weapon systems. Two were used at Treasury Island in October and proved successful. Also converted in-theater were LCI(G)-21, 23, 61, 64–67, and 70, with the addition of another 40mm forward. These were used in the Marshalls at the beginning of 1944. LCIs converted in the States had six different battery configurations (see sidebar). Stateside-converted LCI(G)s were: 2, 17–19, 31*, 34*, 39, 41–43, 46, 61, 68–70, 73*, 77–82, 189, 190, 192, 195, 196, 233–237, 345–348, 365, 366, 372, 373, 396–398, 403–408, 412–415, 417–422, 428, 449–475, 484, 506, 514, 516, 517, 528, 530, 534, 538–542, 556, 558–561, 563, 565–568, 570, 574 (cancelled), 576, 577, 580, 594–596, 630–633†, 638†, 658–660†, 661, 725–730, 739–742†, 751, 752, 754–757†, 760†, 801–810†, 948, 975†, 1010–1012†, 1023†, 1055–1059†, 1088†, and 1089†.[5] Some of these craft were in turn converted to LCI(M)s.

Landing Craft, Infantry (Rocket)

In April 1944, LCI(G)-31, 34, and 73 were converted in-theater to rocket boats with 24 x 4.5in Mk 1 or Mk 8 launcher racks with 600 rockets and

5 * = Later converted to LCI(R). † = Later converted to LCI(M).

LCI(G)-346 and 348 were Type A gunboats armed with 2 x 40mm, 3 x 20mm, and 6 x .50cal guns and 10 x 4.5in Mk 7 rocket launchers. The troop ramps were removed from gunboats. While there were standardized camouflage schemes, it was not uncommon for crews to apply their own – note the differences in the two boats' patterns.

ABOVE LEFT
An LCI(R) salvo-fires its 4.5in rockets in a 30-second shrieking volley, Leyte, 1944. Before reloading, which required 2½ hours, the crew would first inspect for any misfired rockets and discard them over the side.

ABOVE RIGHT
LCI(R)-31 at Samar Island, Philippines, November 1944. The former troop ladder platforms are fitted with 4.5in Mk 8 "egg crate" rocket launchers. The boat appears to be painted solid dark green.

storage for 1,000 more. A 40mm gun was mounted on the forecastle and two 20mm guns on the fantail. Additional boats were temporarily converted in time to be used in the Marshalls at the beginning of 1944 and unofficially designated LCI(FS) – Fire Support: LCI(FS)-77–80, 365, 366, and 437–442. These boats were armed with 6 x 4.5in rocket racks each firing 72 rockets plus 3 x 40mm, 2 x 20mm, and 5 x .50cal guns. Stateside, rocket boats were converted from LCI(L)-351 class boats and from three LCI(G)s, with 36 built in total. Armament was the same as the LCI(M), but 6 x 5in rocket launchers replaced the three mortars. The craft were fitted with a modified aircraft H2C radar to allow them to position themselves precisely. They were also used as radar pickets outside the main fleet area to warn of approaching aircraft. The LCI(R) had the smallest crew of the fire support LCIs: three officers and 31 men. LCI(R)s included: 31*, 34*, 71*–74, 223–226, 230, 331, 337, 338, 340–342, 642–651, 704–708, 762–767, 769–772, 1024, 1026, 1028–1030, 1068–1070, 1077, and 1078.[6]

Landing Craft, Infantry (Mortar)

In 1942, the US Army Chemical Warfare Service experimented with mounting 4.2in chemical mortars on LCIs and LCTs at Amphibious Training Center, Carabelle, FL. The "four-deuce" mortar was intended to deliver chemical and smoke rounds, but since chemical rounds would not be used, high-explosive shells were approved. Able to fire close to shore, the mortars would be able to continue suppressive fire when the naval and aerial bombardments ceased and right up to moment the assault troops came ashore. The mortar induced a heavy recoil and a robust timber frame filled with sand and sawdust was developed to hold the baseplate.

The first combat of seaborne mortars saw them mounted on LCTs during the July 1943 Sicily landing. It was then decided to modify some LCIs specifically as mortar boats, and they saw their first action during the September 1944 Peleliu assault. LCI(M)s were subsequently employed in most other landings in the Pacific, as well at Normandy in June 1944. Forty-two LCI(M)s were built, with many being converted from LCI(G)s. They possessed a single 40mm gun, four 20mm guns, and three 4.2in mortars (two immediately forward of the deckhouse near the gunwales and another on the centerline further forward. A total of 1,200 x 4.2in rounds were carried in what had been the No. 2 troop compartment. The crew was four officers and 49 men. The mortar crews were usually trained by US Army chemical mortar battalions and on some boats the mortars were manned by similarly trained Marines.

6 * = Converted from LCI(G).

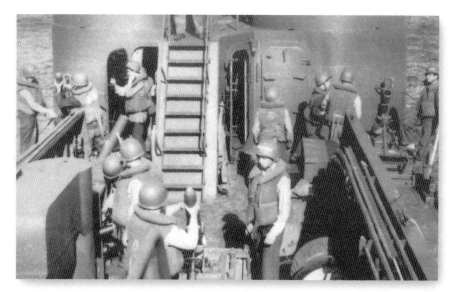

The three 4.2in M2 mortar crews on an LCI(M) prepare to fire ranging rounds as they approach shore. The open hatch on the right side of the deckhouse ladder leads to the ammunition magazine, the former No. 2 troop compartment.

Those vessels designated as LCI(M) were as follows: 351–356*, 359, 362, 431, 437–442, 582, 588, 630–633*, 638*, 658–660*, 664, 669, 670, 673, 674, 739–742*, 754–757*, 760*, 951, 952, 975*, 1010–1012*, 1023*, 1055–1059*, 1088*, and 1089*.[7]

Landing Craft, Support (Large) Mk 3

The final type based on the LCI was the LCS(L)(3), numbered 1–130,[8] known as "Mighty Midgets" and built by three firms after development by the lead company, George Lawley. Construction started at the end of April 1944 and ran through the end of the year. Vessels were built in a remarkably short time, sometimes in three weeks plus another 2–4 weeks for pre-commission fitting. The 158ft LCS(L) was based on the LCI hull, but was greatly reconfigured internally, with an entirely different superstructure and deck arrangement. Its LCI origins were barely recognizable, although it retained the "castle bridge," but the deckhouse was further forward. This was basically a gunboat designed for near-shore fire support and interdicting inter-island barge traffic. There were no gangways or bow doors, but the craft could be beached to provide a stable firing platform for inland targets, something seldom done. Inside were storage compartments, magazines, crew quarters, officers' quarters, officers' mess, crew mess and more crew quarters, generator room, refrigerators, engine room with eight General Motors diesels (four per shaft), ordnance stores, workshop, magazines, storage, and steering gear. On the bow was a tub for a 3in or

A stern quarter view of an LCS(L)(3). The small elevated tub forward of the aft 40mm is for the fire control director, but these were never installed owing to shortages. The steam clouds are caused by the discharge of hot engine coolant water into cold seawater.

7 * = Converted from LCI(G)s.

8 The LCS(L) Mk 1 and 2 were British 47ft and 105ft fire support craft. The LCS(R) was a 145ft British rocket-firing craft of an entirely different design.

ABOVE
Haze gray-painted LCS(L)(3)-22, with a banged-up bow. Such damage was common owing to inexperienced crews and the solid resistance of docks. The running-light mast fitted on the front of the twin 40mm tub was removed when in action.

ABOVE RIGHT
LCS(L)(3)-12 painted haze gray. This is a post-war photo. The four 20mm guns have been removed, although the mounts remain.

RIGHT
LCS(L)(3)-129 is fitted with twin 40mm guns on the bow, forward of the pilothouse, and on the fantail. The projecting tub on the front of the bridge is for an uninstalled 40mm gun director.

LCS(L)(3) characteristics	
Dimensions	
Length:	158ft ½in
Beam:	23ft 3in
Displacement	
Loaded:	387 tons
Landing:	312 tons
Light:	250 tons
Draft	
Loaded:	4ft 9in forward, 6ft 6in aft
Landing:	3ft 10in forward, 5ft 8in aft
Light:	4ft mean
Speed	
Maximum:	15½ knots
Endurance	
12 knots:	5,500 miles

single 40mm or twin 40mm guns.[9] Most had 10 x 4.5in Mk 7 launcher racks (two sets of five) on the forward deck. On the forward portion of the deckhouse was a twin 40mm and there was another on the fantail. Inside the deckhouse were heads, washroom, chart and radio room, and galley. Centered was the pilothouse with the conn and gun directors above this. A 20mm gun was mounted on either side of the pilothouse with two more just aft of the deckhouse. Complement was five officers and 65 men. While this version was based on the LCI(L), the significant design changes altered its characteristics much more than the other LCI fire support variants. On February 28, 1949, the remaining LSC(L)(3)s were reclassified as Landing Ship, Support (Large) – LSS(L). Fifty-three were transferred to the Japanese Maritime Self-Defense Force in 1952.

LANDING SHIP, MEDIUM

To provide a vehicle-carrying landing ship with seagoing capabilities similar to the LCI, the LSM was developed in 1944 and built in six different yards. LSMs were typically launched in three weeks, with another three weeks necessary for fitting. The type used features of the LST and LCT(6), and while under development was called LCT(7). The first vessels were ordered as such

9 Vessels armed with 3in gun: LCS(L)-1–10, 26–30, 41–50, 58–60, 79, and 80; single 40mm gun: 11–25, 31–40, 51–57, 61–66, 81–89, and 109–124; twin 40mm guns: 67–78, 92–108, and 125–130.

and assigned hull numbers in the 1500–1800 LCT series, but were renumbered when reclassified as LSMs.

The LSM was 40ft longer than its LCI troop-carrying counterpart and 11ft broader – 203ft 6in long, 34ft 6in beam. Speed though was 2–3 knots less than an LCI. It could carry five light or three medium tanks, or six amphibious Landing Vehicle, Tracked (LVT) vehicles (better known as "amtracs"), or nine DUKW ("Duck") amphibious trucks plus 54 passengers; later accommodation was for 48 passengers. Alternatively, it could carry 150 tons of bulk cargo. The LVTs and Ducks could be launched and retrieved at sea via the bow ramp. The complement was four officers and 48 men, later increased to 54 men.

A vehicle well deck ran the entire length, from the double bow doors and 16ft 2in long ramp to the stern plate, which could be removed. This facility allowed any number of LSMs to be moored end-to-end to serve as a causeway, allowing vehicles to be driven from LSTs to the beach. The deck's width varied. The opening to the ramp was 14ft wide, but then widened out to 22ft 8in for about a third of the deck's length and then narrowed again to 18ft for almost 90ft. The aft-most portion was 12ft wide for 17ft. On either side were high compartmented bulkheads. On the port side, from bow to stern, were machinery, storage, hospital, galley, engine access hatches, and workshop compartments; the compartments were only 5–7ft wide. On the well deck's port side in the immediate stern was the stern anchor winch under a platform. The bow anchor was on the forward port side. On the starboard side were machinery, head, washroom, heating boiler, and ordnance stores compartments. Beneath the tank deck were ballast tanks; crew, officer and troop quarters; storage, refrigerator and machinery compartments; engine room, fuel tanks, and more troop and storage compartments, with steering

ABOVE
LSM(R)-194 in the South Pacific camouflage scheme. While the colors were predominately green shades, on the stern quarters there was usually a large black splotch, as here.

BELOW LEFT
The forward side of LSM-275's pilothouse. It was not uncommon for vessels to display colorful insignia. LSM-275 was converted to a cable-laying and repair ship, USS *Portunus* (ARC-1), in 1952.

BELOW RIGHT
The deck levels, main compartments, armament, and features of an LSM as depicted on a Navy chart.

gear in the lazarette. The two Fairbanks-Morse Model 38D8 or General Motors Cleveland Model 16-278A diesel engines each gave 1,440hp. Early ships had a 7,000-mile range and later 4,900 miles at 12 knots.

Atop the side bulkhead structures were three pairs of 20mm gun tubs, three per side: two just aft of the bow ramp compartment (later replaced by a single or twin 40mm tub on the forecastle platform bridging over the bow ramp compartment), two just forward of amidships, and two more near the fantail. Just abaft of the amidships starboard 20mm was the deckhouse with chartroom and radio room, topped by the pilothouse, and that by the conn. Just aft of the bridge was accommodation for a 3ft-wide removable catwalk allowing access to the port side bulkhead deck. In total, 525 LSMs were built, with all serving in the Pacific: LSM-1–187, 200–400, 413–500, and 537–588. Seven were lost. LSM-161, 226, 419, and 546 served in the Korean War. LSM-161 was the last of the type in service, finishing its days in 1965 as a logistics support ship in the Aleutians: USS *Kodiak*.

LSM-549 and 550–552 were reclassified as salvage lifting vessels (ARSD-1–4) before they were laid down at the war's end. Much redesignated, they were commissioned in December 1945 as USS *Gypsy*, *Mender*, *Salvager*, and *Windlass*, respectively. They were decommissioned in the 1940s through the 1960s. Many LSMs were transferred or sold to Denmark, Greece, South Korea, Norway, Republic of China, Spain, Thailand, Turkey, South Vietnam, Venezuela, and other Latin American countries through the 1940s, 1950s, and 1960s. They may have served as landing ships or have been converted to coastal minelayers (MMC) or to other auxiliaries.

Landing Ship, Medium (Rocket)

There were two classes of LSM (Rocket), both known as a "Whoofus" – US Army troops were said to ask: "Whoofus this boat supposed to be?" The tank deck was provided with an overhead for a new main deck on which the rocket launchers were mounted. The side bulkhead compartments remained much the same as on the LSM, as did the former lower deck with the troop compartments accommodating the enlarged crew. The former tank deck was compartmentalized with rocket motor and rocket body (with warhead) magazines and rocket assembly rooms. LSM(R) vessels were also

E **LSM AND LSM(R)**

1: All LSMs served in the Pacific and while usually painted haze gray with blue decks, including the well deck, they were often painted in green camouflage schemes. While the ideal bow armament was twin 40mm guns, many were armed with a single 40mm on a platform over the ramp compartment and even more had a 20mm tub just abaft the forecastle (see insert). Regardless of the forward armament, all LSMs had two more 20mm guns amidships and two on the fantail.

2: The LSM(R)-188 class was a relatively quick conversion of an LSM to a rocket and gunboat vessel accomplished by decking over the well deck and dividing the interior into numerous compartments. There were two variations of 5in rocket armament. LSM(R)-188–195 had 75 x Mk 36 and 30 x Mk 30 rocket launchers, while LSM(R)-196–199 had 85 x Mk 51 launchers, shown here. Both types had a bow 40mm gun, another forward of the pilothouse, a 5in gun on the fantail, and three 20mm guns. The small elevated tub forward of the 5in gun mounts the fire director.

3: Most 401 class rocket boats were painted a dark gray with a black bottom side. This was a complete redesign, still based on the LSM hull, but it had a completely different superstructure on the stern, with the 5in gun just forward and 10 x twin 5in Mk 102 rocket launchers forward. Other armament included twin 40mms on the bow and fantail, 4 x twin 20mms and 4 x 4.2in mortars, plus two .50cal and two .30cal machine guns. Pacific Fleet 1944 directives stated that the bow and stern quarter hull number of large landing craft and landing ships would be 4ft high. On LCIs and LSMs the stern quarter number height was 4ft, often extending to 6ft.

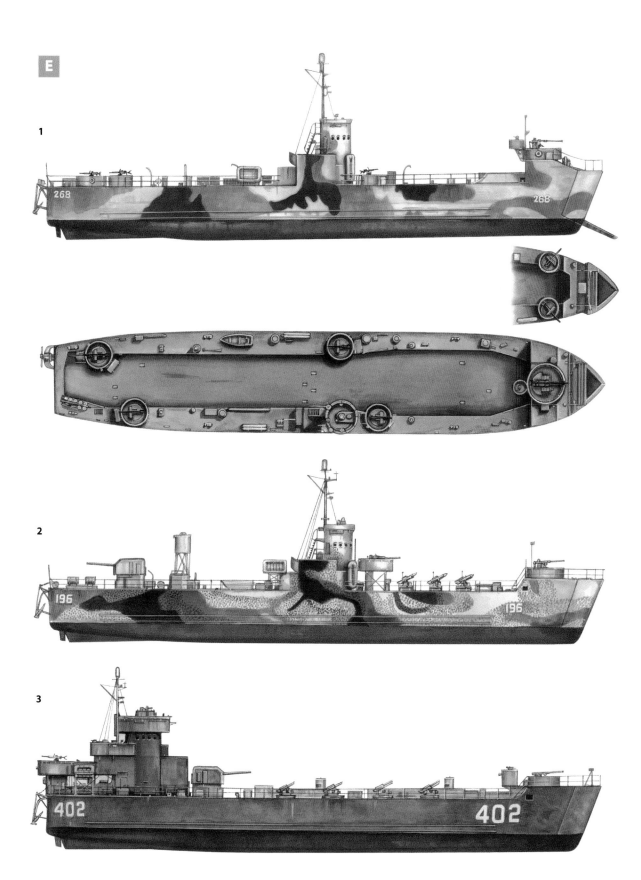

This picture of LSM-32 moored alongside LCI(L)-992 provides an idea of the size difference between the two vessels. They are moored inside ABSD-6, a large auxiliary floating dry dock (ten-section, non-self-propelled) at Guam.

equipped with radar and used as radar pickets. They were considered the ultimate fire support vessels and would replace all LCI-based fire support craft after the war.

The LSM(R)-188 class retained the LCM's starboard superstructure. These were built between August and October 1944. There was a single 40mm on the bow, an elevated 40mm tub forward of the pilothouse, a 20mm abeam the superstructure on the port side and two 20mms near the stern. A 5in (38cal) gun in a destroyer-type turret was mounted on the fantail. LSM(R)-188–195 mounted 75 four-rail Mk 36 and 30 six-rail Mk 30 5in rocket racks. LSM(R)-196–199 mounted automatic-feed 5in Mk 51 rocket launchers and were 40 tons heavier. The crew was five officers and 76 men. Four of the 12 LSM(R)-188 class were lost at Okinawa.

The 48 LSM(R)-401 class ships were of a much different arrangement, with the lower deck reconfigured with rocket magazines and a different crew quarters layout. This class included LSM(R)-401–412 and 501–536 built between early 1945 and the summer. The last 36 of the 501 subclass had minor differences from the 401 class. The second deck was also rearranged, with rocket assembly and handling rooms and additional crew quarters for the six officers and 137 men. A somewhat larger centerline deckhouse was

BELOW LEFT
LSM(R)-193 rocket ship with its six-rail Mk 36 and four-rail Mk 30 5in rocket launchers empty. It required 2½ hours to reload the second barrage and 4½ hours for a subsequent barrage owing to the less convenient stowage, as rockets had to be manhandled to deck through multiple compartments further aft.

BELOW RIGHT
The differences between the LSM(R)-401 class and the LSM(R)-188 class are apparent. The deckhouse was on the fantail with the 5in gun turret forward and it mounted 10 x 5in automatic-feed Mk 103 twin rocket launchers.

LSM(R)-195 being launched in October 1944 at the Charleston Navy Yard, SC. As can be seen, a great deal of work remained to be accomplished before completion and commissioning a few weeks later.

built just forward of the fantail. It held a radar and rocket control room, wardroom, galley, and mess at main deck level. Above these was the radio and chart room, over which was situated the bridge, on top of which was a tub for a 2.5m optical rangefinder and rocket director. Armament was much changed as well, with a twin 40mm on the bow, twin 20mm tubs just to the aft on either side, plus two more on either side of the deckhouse. A 5in turreted gun was immediately forward of the deckhouse.

The fantail 5in gun of the LSM(R)-188 class required the ship to turn broadside to shore to fire and so presented a broadside target. Mounting a 5in forward of the deckhouse on the LSM(R)-401 class allowed this to be fired as the vessel advanced toward shore. Mounted atop the winch room on the fantail was a twin 40mm tub. Four 4.2in mortars were provided, two forward of the deckhouse and one on either side. Two .50cal machine guns were mounted on the forecastle and two .30cal machine guns on bridge wings. Ten 5in Mk 102 twin automatic rocket launchers were mounted on the forward deck. The goal was to provide an all-purpose fire support vessel with rockets, guns, and mortars. None saw action in World War II, but they would have been employed for the invasion of Japan.

After the war, some LSM(R)s were rearmed with twin-tube continuous-feed 5in Mk 105 launchers. These were fed by automatic hoists with a load of 380 improved rockets, and the mortars were removed from all the vessels. These modifications allowed the crew to be reduced to five officers and 76 men. After the war most were mothballed. Eight saw service in the Korean War with Rocket Division 32 – LSM(R)-401, 403, 404, 409, 412, 525, 527, and 536 – and were returned to mothballs after the war. On October 1, 1955, the 48 remaining ships were named after rivers (exclusive of rivers bearing state names, to prevent confusion with battleships). In 1965 LSM(R)-409, 525, and 536 were recommissioned – USS *Clarion River*, *Saint Francis River*, and *White River*, respectively – for Vietnam service with Inshore Fire Support Division 93. LSM(R)-401, 404, 405, 409, 412, 512, 513, 515, 522, 525, 531, and 536 were reclassified as inshore fire support ships (LFR) on January 1, 1969 – a moot point as all had been decommissioned by 1970, never to serve again.

OPERATIONAL HISTORY

LCIs, LSMs, and their fire support variants played important but often unheralded roles in the new form of large-scale amphibious warfare.[10] LCIs of all types fought in all major theaters. In the Pacific they served from the Aleutian Islands to the Netherlands East Indies, and were prepared to strike at Japan. They operated in far northern waters with the Red Fleet and in the Mediterranean and English Channel with the US Navy and Royal Navy. Their missions were varied and often dangerous, as can be seen in the summary below.

LCI and LSM units

Landing vessel units were organized into flotillas, groups, and divisions in descending echelons usually commanded by a captain, commander, and lieutenant-commander, respectively. (It was not uncommon for the various commanders to be a rank lower than those here given.) An LCIFlot of 24 boats was organized into two groups of two divisions, each with six boats. As an example, LCIFlot 4 with LCI(L)s 83–96, 319–326, 349, and 350 consisted of LCIGrps 7 and 8 with LCIDivs 13–16. The LCIFlot 4 flagship was LCI-87 and the two LCIGrp flagships were LCI-89 and 321. The division commander was simply the senior LCI skipper in each division and had no additional staff. LSM flotillas were organized the same.

LCI(G), LCI(M), and LCS(L) flotillas had three groups of two divisions each, six boats per division for a total of 36 in the flotilla. The LCI(R) flotilla could be under this organization or have only two groups for a total of 24 rocket boats. They usually operated as groups or divisions when conducting fire missions and even in pairs or single ships when patrolling or providing post-landing fire support.

How LCIs were incorporated into the landing force varied from operation to operation. The flotilla organization was mainly administrative in nature. When a landing force was organized, LCI flotillas were broken up and the ships assigned to task groups and task units. Flotilla, group, and division commanders might be assigned as task group and unit

LSM-14 wearing dapple-pattern camouflage. Most LSMs had a pair of 20mm guns on the bow. Later ships had a bridged-over forecastle mounting a 40mm gun. With the ramp raised and the doors closed, the space between the ramp and the V-shaped space of the outer doors could be flooded to waterline level and used by the crew for bathing.

10 See Osprey Elite 117: *US World War II Amphibious Tactics: Pacific Theater* and Elite 144: *US World War II Amphibious Tactics: European and Mediterranean Theaters.*

F

LCI(R) ROCKET FIRING

LCI(G)-73 was first converted to a gunboat and then a rocket boat along with LCI-31 and 34 in the Pacific. She participated in 14 operations, first as a troop-carrier and then as a fire support boat. Here she bears a locally created camouflage scheme. In her early Type F LCI(G) gunboat configuration she mounted more rocket launchers than most rocket boats: 24 x 4.5in Mk 1 racks, each holding 12 rockets. The aft six launchers on each side are being fired in the first barrage about 1,000yd from shore and the forward launchers will be fired a few hundred yards closer to the beach to impact in the same area just behind the dune line. Additional armament included a bow 40mm and three 20mm guns.

LCI(L)-1 class boats en route to Normandy with very-low-altitude (VLA) barrage balloons tethered. After they were moved ashore upon landing, it was found that the Germans used the balloons as artillery aiming points and they were all eventually cut loose.

LCIs were notorious for rolling and yawing in even moderate seas, which made them no friend of their passengers. This view is looking forward on an LCI(L)-1 class boat.

commanders as well as command elements and divisions within the task organization, which might mean commanding other types of landing craft in the mixed organization, including LSMs, LCTs, and LCMs. Such organizations might be called attack groups, landing and control craft groups, landing craft groups, beach groups (preceded by the beach color designation), assault groups, or reserve groups. As an example, for the Sicily landing, the Licata Attack Force (TF 80) contained the Gaffi Attack Group (TG 86.2) with 7 x LSTs, 15 x LCIs, and 21 x LCTs, plus the Falconara Attack Group (TG 86.5) with 10 x LSTs, 16 x LCIs, and 9 x LCTs. There were also four other task groups assigned to TF 80 with additional LSTs, landing craft, fire support ships, transports, etc. Such groups were divided into waves, with LCIs coming in after the immediate beachhead was secure to deliver reserve battalions and combat support units. Not all missions were combat assaults. LCIs and LSMs were commonly used for various mundane tasks: shuttling passengers, vehicles, and cargo from base to base; lightering personnel, cargo and vehicles ashore from troop and cargo ships; resupplying units as they advanced along the coast; and simply providing ferry services.

Fire support missions

The primary mission of LCI gunboats, mortar boats and rocket boats, LCS gunboats, and LSM rocket boats was to provide preparatory and suppressive fire support to amphibious tractor and landing boat groups making the initial assault. They would continue to provide fire support throughout the later phases of an amphibious operation.

The operational duties of the fire support vessels during an amphibious landing included:

- Protecting the amtrac or boat group from enemy automatic weapons fire from the beach and from enemy aircraft while in the rendezvous area, en route to the landing zone, and at the line of departure.
- Supporting the landing of the assault waves with rocket, mortar, and/or automatic weapons fire in order to neutralize the enemy beach defenses.
- Supporting the troops after landing and during the boat shuttle movement by directing fire against enemy positions on the beach and against enemy aircraft.
- Laying such smoke screens as may be ordered to hinder enemy observation and fire control, by means of smoke rockets and fog generators.
- Assisting UDTs by covering them with supporting fire or smoke (when ordered) in order to permit the accomplishment of reconnaissance and demolitions.
- Making false demonstrations when ordered, using gunfire, rocket fire, and smoke in order to divert the enemy away from the main landing or make him suspect another landing will occur elsewhere.
- Performing direct support and harassing missions in support of the troops after the landing and until the completion of the operation. This included direct fire support for troops operating along the shore.
- Providing antiaircraft screens for radar pickets.
- Providing "flycatcher" screens against suicide boats and swimmers.
- Performing radar countermeasures, when ordered (when so equipped).

Other missions commonly assigned to fire support craft included: search and interdiction patrols for enemy barge traffic attempting resupply, counterlandings, and casualty evacuation; rescuing crews from sinking landing vessels and ships; recovering downed airmen, both friendly and enemy; patrolling the perimeter of ship anchorages; conducting reconnaissance patrols up navigable rivers and along remote coastlines; and other odd missions.

The tactics employed by fire support craft depended on multiple factors: the width of the landing beach; available craft and their types (rocket, gun, mortar); types and dispersion of enemy fortifications; expected enemy

A *kamikaze* slammed into this LCI(R), but the explosion failed to detonate the hundreds of 5in spin-stabilized rocket warheads. LCIs were not known for their ability to sustain and survive such catastrophic damage. This one was fortunate.

35

Rocket Boat Fire Plan
This example of a firing plan for 4.5in rocket-armed boats depicts six LCI(R or G) or LSM(R) commencing fire at 2,000yd with 40mm guns, firing ranging rockets at 1,800yd, launching the first salvo set at 45 degrees, elevation at 1,600–1,800yd, the second salvo set at 30 degrees at 1,130yd, and turning to the flanks at 960yd. The Line of Departure is where the amtracs/assault boats assembled. M.P.I. = Mean Point of Impact.

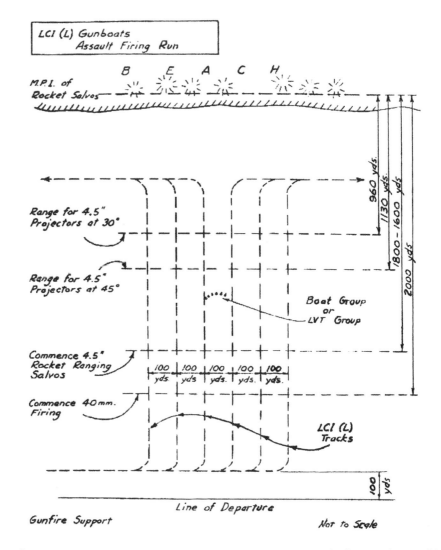

firepower; terrain and vegetation; timing of air support; whether smoke would be employed; wind and current conditions; composition of the assault waves; and other conditions. In the Mediterranean and European theaters, the assault landing was conducted by several waves of LCVPs, with LCMs and LCTs in the follow-on waves. In the Pacific, after the November 1943 Tarawa assault, most landing assault waves were delivered by amphibious tractors, often led by amphibious tanks. Later waves of support elements, tanks, and artillery would land by LCVP, LCM, LCT, and Ducks. Some landings in the Philippines, however, were made without amtracs if little or no resistance was expected.

Typically the fire support craft would form line abreast 100yd ahead of the amtrac/assault boat line of departure, being positioned at 100yd intervals. Four to eight vessels could be assigned to each landing beach – six a was common number. They then proceeded toward the beach, covering the assault waves with 40mm and 20mm automatic weapons fire. This purely suppressive fire actually hit little, but created a great deal of noise, dust, and rapid explosions, plus a spectacular tracer display. The fire helped keep the enemy's heads down, created confusion, added to the shock effects of the general bombardment, and degraded morale while greatly improving the assault troops' confidence. At 1,000yd range, the fire support craft armed with the shorter-ranged

4.5in rockets commenced their rocket barrage and ceased at 500yd or more, dependent on the width of the fringing reef if in the Pacific. (Some reefs were further offshore, but landing beaches were usually selected in areas with narrower reefs.) The craft armed with the longer-ranged 5in rocket first fired individual ranging rockets further from shore as they closed in. When the rockets began impacting in the designated target area the craft then fired mass ripple barrages. The range of the 5in rockets was also useful if wide reefs were present.

The US Navy's rendition of the loss of LCI(L)-93 on deadly Omaha Beach, Normandy, June 1944. Grounded, the boat was battered by German artillery.

Groups of rocket launchers on a given boat were usually set at two different elevations, and were fired in two separate barrages at specific ranges to allow both barrages to impact in the same area. Timing was everything. The fire plan called for the rocket and mortar fire to be laid down as the naval gunfire lifted. Mortar boats also fired ranging rounds until they ranged in on the target area. The mortar boats might be given more specific targets than rocket boats, but they were still only marginally accurate area fire weapons.

At the 500yd (or more) ceasefire line, the fire support vessels would sometimes turn to the flanks to clear the way for the assault craft, while at other times they would lie dead in the water to continue providing automatic weapons fire. This latter option required them to constantly adjust their propeller thrust to counter wave, current, and wind action to remain in position. It was a dangerous, stationary tactic. While LCIs and LSMs were not in the initial assault waves, they were exposed to fire from shore, including coast defense guns, artillery, mortars, and automatic cannons as well as air attack. In the Pacific they experienced *kamikaze* attacks, even though larger vessels made more tempting targets for the enemy aircraft. Damage-control training was crucial.

The amtrac or landing craft waves would soon pass through. Usually, after the amtrac/boat waves passed and before they hit the beach, the fire support craft vacated the assault lanes by proceeding in column to the flanks so that follow-on waves had a clear approach. They took up station and fired on

areas flanking the landing beach and sometimes deeper targets. Crew drill and fire procedures were important for fire support craft to ensure accurate and timely fire. A major danger was engaging friendly troops when providing post-landing fire support. To prevent friendly fire casualties, the gunships avoided overhead fire after the troops landed and had to be aware of the land advance along the shore to the flanks. The 3in and 5in guns were not used for general area fire as automatic weapons were – they were reserved for identifiable point targets. It did little good merely to fire slow-rate weapons blindly at an island; they had to fire at specific point targets (pillboxes, gun positions, etc) to do any good.

For the many other follow-on missions assigned them, the fire support ships usually operated in units of 2–4 craft. The fire support group would rotate units to allow them to refuel, rearm, and reposition. This rotation also allowed crews to get some rest, as when in the firing line all hands were continuously at general quarters (manning battle stations on full alert). They typically visited destroyers and transports, "bumming" rations, fresh water, fuel, and 20mm and 40mm ammunition. On radar picket anti-aircraft screen duty, four boats usually formed a station and maneuvered around a tight square offering each other maximum anti-aircraft cover. "Flycatcher" screening missions protected transport anchorages from nighttime suicide boats and swimmers. They patrolled the perimeters in irregular patterns and at all times, maintaining a high degree of vigilance and always prepared to open fire with automatic weapons and star shells.

Landing missions

Life was different for LCIs and LSMs. They practiced landing and debarkation operations under flotilla control. Beaching required skill to prevent broaching – when the vessel turned broadside to waves, current, and winds, resulting in

LCS(L)(3)-50 fire support craft. She mounts a 3in gun on the bow, twin 40mm cannon on the forward end of the deckhouse and the fantail, two 20mm cannon on either side of the bridge, two more just aft of the deckhouse, and two groups of five 4.5in Mk 7 launchers forward of the deckhouse, here covered by canvas shrouds.

unretractable beaching. Other demands included identifying landmarks and beach markers in order to beach in the correct area, timing when to drop the stern anchor, preventing collisions with other beaching craft, and avoiding obstacles and wreckage. Self-retraction was also a complex affair. Tension had to be maintained on the stern anchor to keep it taut, varying the two propellers' speeds separately to "wiggle" off the beach, all the while avoiding breaching and collisions with other vessels and obstacles. Ship commanders might also drag the bow anchor as they backed off to prevent the bow from swinging into adjacent craft as the bow found water.

After depositing follow-on troops, the landing craft conducted endless support missions, bringing in more troops, vehicles, and cargo, as well as escorting and navigating for convoys of smaller landing craft. Crews were spared unloading cargo. That was the responsibility of shore party stevedores and vehicle crews, although the boat's crew had to clean up any mess left behind. A rule of thumb for unloading an LCI was that 25 stevedores were needed.

Troops debark as they emerge from the No. 2 troop compartment on a 351 class boat. Other troops had previously debarked from No. 1 compartment, emerging from beneath the forecastle platform. The beach gradient is such that the troops have to wade some distance to shore.

LCIs on Rendova Island in the New Georgia Group, July 1943. LCI-24 and 65 are listing due to splinter damage from a Japanese bomb that detonated between them. Troops are still unloading cargo.

As already noted, the LCI(L)-1 class could realistically accommodate troops for only 48 hours owing to limited mess, sanitation, and berthing facilities. The LCI(L)-351 class had a longer endurance. If the troops were to be on board for only 24 hours, it could carry 223 men. For no more than 48 hours, it could handle 185 men. For extended operations for between six and eight days it could accommodate 173 men. In all three cases, nine troop officers could be accommodated. There were unopposed short runs of a few hours duration, when up to 350 men were transported on a single LCI. Training on radio and other means of communications was emphasized, as coordination and communication of orders and changes were essential. Anti-aircraft gunnery was also critical and practiced often.

The crews

LCI and LSM crews, including those of the fire support variants, first received their specialty training at various US Navy schools across the country. They were assembled at Amphibious Training Base, Little Creek, VA. There they were assigned to crew and undertook combined training, which included gunnery training and training in other specialties' duties.

A boat had at least three officers: the commander – typically a lieutenant (junior grade) – and an executive officer and engineer officer, both ensigns. Additional officers on fire support boats were usually billeted as communications, gunnery or watch officers, but they typically had multiple duties. The enlisted crew varied in strength and ratings. There were petty officers in charge of the different departments (deck, engineering, gunnery,

G **LCI DEBARKING TROOPS**

The LCI was a troop landing vessel intended for deploying follow-on waves after the initial beachhead was secured by assault troops that had been landed by small landing craft or amphibious tractors. Both the LCI(L)-1 class and 351 class boats, the former depicted here, relied on 2ft 6in-wide gangway ramps, 28ft long for the 1 class and 32ft for the 351 class. Troops had to descend single file and were rather exposed. The I-beam catheads supporting the raising and lowering block-and-tackle were pivoted inboard when not in use. Ramps were lost to heavy surf, damaged by gunfire or collisions, and tangled in wreckage. There were alternative means of debarking. Two scaling ladders were stowed horizontally on the outboard side of the bulwark. These could be placed over the bow forward of the ramp catheads or anywhere over the sides. They might be "borrowed" by infantrymen to climb seawalls or low cliffs fronting the beach, or to bridge barbed wire barriers. Landing nets could also be dropped over the sides of the bow to allow troops to climb down.

An LCI flotilla docked at Bizerte, Tunisia, in July 1943 embarks troops for the Sicily invasion. There was a shortage of troop transports and small landing craft for the invasion. The LCIs performed valuable service by lifting follow-on reserve units. The main assault troops were mostly carried aboard LSTs, each equipped with six small landing craft.

signals, supply, etc.). Ratings included motor machinist's mates, pharmacist's mates, steward's mates, boatswain's mates, radiomen, radarmen, coxswains, quartermasters, and seamen. The latter did the deck work and manned the armament. If a boat had a full crew, however, it was considered fortunate.

The shakedown cruise of a new boat conducted by the commissioning crew served to put the boat through its paces and train the crew as well as bind them into a close-knit team. Once assigned to a boat, crew members more often remained with it through their service. Crews typically developed a firm bond and would remain lifelong shipmates. Most of these vessels were manned by Navy Reservists, that is, mostly conscripted sailors, but 28 LCI(L)s were manned by Coast Guardsmen.[11] The officers too were Navy Reservists; graduates of Annapolis (home of the United States Naval Academy) were seldom assigned to small craft.

11 Coast Guard LCIs were assigned to LCIFlot 4, later redesignated LCIFlot 10 then 35. The Coast Guard was under Navy jurisdiction from November 1941 to January 1946.

Combat-loaded troops debark from LCI(L)-326 in the Mediterranean, either at Sicily or Salerno. The hull plates soon took on a rippled appearance from wave pounding. Thinner hull plating was used on LCIs than on LSTs.

Early use in the Pacific

The first use of LCIs in the Pacific was during the June 1943 New Georgia Group landings. Owing to construction and training delays, it was a near thing that LCIFlot 5's 26 boats arrived in time to participate in planning and rehearsals. They first required two weeks of maintenance and repairs. En route to the objective, a severe storm forced the LCIs to reduce their speed from 12 to 8.5 knots in the head-on seas. The landings were successfully executed and the LCIs delivered troops of the second and fourth echelons. They had a hard time, though, with a twisting approach route among the small scattered islands, difficult currents, and mud beaches. It was later learned that five Japanese destroyers had tried to intercept them in the dark. Two LCIs collided during course changes, although with little damage. Aircraft strafing attacks were endured by the second-echelon boats, but 16 bombers attacked the fourth echelon and three LCIs were damaged, but still sailable. The LCIs had the satisfaction of downing a few of the attackers with anti-aircraft guns. While LSTs were employed in the operation, the smaller LCIs were able to get into more inaccessible beaches to discharge their troops and cargo. They also proved valuable for delivering small landing forces in remote island areas.

LCIs assault Sicily

There were serious landing craft shortages for the July 1943 Sicily landings. Only LCI(L)-1 class boats intended for short passages were available. The assault battalion of each of the infantry regiments was landed by Landing Craft, Vehicle and Personnel (LCVP) launched from LSTs. The second battalion may have been landed by LCVPs or LCTs and in some instances by LCIs, a mission for which they were not intended. The third battalions may have been landed by LCIs or LCTs.

This first use of LCIs in the Mediterranean so early in the assault violated their envisioned employment, but it was a matter of necessity. The landings were conducted at several widely separated points. LCIs at Licata on the US left flank had a particularly hard time. The pre-dawn landing of the initial assault waves alerted the defenders and it was not long before German bombers arrived to pummel the follow-on waves. The landing craft

LSM-152 in the Pacific dappled camouflage scheme, in predominately green shades. The well deck was most likely painted deck green, a dark green color.

had already endured heavy weather and barely arrived on time. Running the gauntlet of bursting bombs, they soon encountered artillery and machine-gun fire. Several LCIs were damaged and suffered casualties. One grounded on a false beach (an offshore sandbar) and had to transfer its troops to another vessel. A beaching LCI gunned down an Italian soldier about to throw a grenade onto its deck just yards away. Other LCIs hammered pillboxes with 20mm fire to have the occupants rush out to surrender. One LCI with a regimental commander aboard beached in an area of concentrated fire – one ramp was ripped off by the surf and the other fouled with another LCI. The skipper intentionally broached his craft and the troops were forced to drop over the side. Some drowned in the pounding surf. Regardless of the opposition and surf conditions, the LCI crews managed to get the troops ashore in the dark, with very limited fire support.

Rocket boats at Kwajalein

The 7th Infantry Division's January 1944 assault on Kwajalein in the Marshall Islands was led by 12 rocket-firing LCI(FS)s. These were standard LCIs temporarily fitted out as rocket boats with six racks firing a total of 600 x 4.5in rockets. Assigned to Fire Support Group 4 (Task Group 52.8) along with four battleships, three heavy cruisers, and ten destroyers, they were additionally assigned to Fire Support Unit 4 (Task Unit 52.8.4) and divided equally between LCI(FS) Divisions 13 and 15.

The first phase of the operation was to seize two small islands northwest of the main objective, Kwajalein. These were Ennylabegan (codenamed CARLOS) and Enubuj (CARLSON). Each of the two LCI(FS) divisions was assigned an island and went in ahead of the amtracs, ripping loose with 3,600 rockets onto each island. Of particular note after the devastating rocket barrage was the 40mm, 20mm, and .50cal fire provided by the LCIs, which went close in to the beaches after the attack waves. This support was frequently mentioned in the after-action reports of the assault troops. The next day the main assault was unleashed on Kwajalein and the same LCI(FS)s provided support, firing their first barrage at 1,100yd from shore and the second at 800yd. They then opened fire with their automatic weapons right

LSM-20 was struck by a *kamikaze* in Surigao Strait between Leyte and Mindanao on December 5, 1944. Two crewmen can be seen about to jump. LCI(G)-1017 is standing by to rescue the crew. The plane struck aft of the pilothouse on the starboard side just above the waterline. The bombs exploded in the engine room. Eight crew were killed and nine wounded.

up to seconds before the assault troops leapt from their amtracs. The success of these rocket boats, and 12 more supporting the Marine assault on Roi-Namur to the north at the same time, were instrumental in prompting the go-ahead for the conversion of many more fire support boats in the States. The procedures they developed were used throughout the rest of the war.

LSM-24 and 135 beached on e Shima off Okinawa, April 1945. LST-1326 can be seen further down the beach. It was not uncommon for soldiers transported in an LSM to later say they had been aboard an LST, the latter becoming almost a generic name for large landing vessels.

LSMs at Ormoc

In early December 1944, US Eighth Army forces on Leyte were landing units in Ormoc Bay on the island's west side as other units fought their way over the mountains from the east. The Japanese were using Ormoc Bay to reinforce and resupply their battered forces. LSMs rather than LSTs were employed to land supplies and heavy equipment, due to the shallow waters, plus the "Large Slow Targets" were more tempting targets for the relentless *kamikazes*. The suicide fighters attacked in waves and the first victim was LSM-20 as the group of eight LSMs and three LCIs, shielded by destroyers and air cover, made its dash for the landing site. Despite the crew's best efforts to save her, LSM-20 went down. LSM-34 and 23 were damaged by other attackers and LSM-18 took the latter under tow and departed the area. The remaining four LSMs and the LCIs continued toward their destination. The *kamikazes* shifted to attacking the destroyers. One was damaged and taken in tow by an LSM.

Two days after this grueling mission, a second landing was made employing 11 LSMs, 27 LCIs, four LSTs, and eight destroyer-transports. The convoy made it to its objective beach without any attacks. The first two waves were delivered by LCVPs followed by two waves of LCIs, and then one of LSMs. *Kamikazes* appeared and soon sank an LSM, and repeated bombing attacks were made on two more landing craft, but these managed to take effective evasive maneuvers. It was a rough four days, but the LSMs and LCIs were instrumental in outflanking the Japanese and securing the first island to be liberated in the Philippines.

LCI(G)-67 beached at Okinawa after a typhoon. This was a Southwest Pacific gunboat conversion mounting a 40mm, a 3in and four 20mm guns, and six .50cal machine guns.

LCI(M)s at Okinawa

Forty-two LCI(M)s were employed to support the initial assault landing on Okinawa on April 1, 1945, along with LCI rocket ships and gunboats. The 126 mortars laid down a barrage of 28,000 rounds over a strip 5½ miles wide by 300yd deep in less than an hour. Through the remainder of the three-month operation, the mortar boats provided counterbattery and harassing fires along both of the large island's lengthy coasts. In other operations, the mortar boats had not "shot in" the assault waves as did rocket boats, but were on-call in reserve for special missions. Since LCI(M)s lacked radar and had only minimal navigation equipment, they steamed in an elliptical track around a radar-equipped reference ship, a destroyer for example, that kept station by

Passing beneath the Golden Gate bridge, the war-battered LCI(G)-23 returns home after VJ-Day. After being bomb-damaged at Rendova, it was one of the first in-theater LCIs converted to a gunboat.

radar. When on the path of the ellipse and headed toward the island, the reference ship would radio range and azimuth (direction) to the mortar boats and they would fire when aligned with the target. The 4.2in mortar rounds generated a heavy blast effect – a 4.2in (107mm) high-explosive projectile contained 8lb of TNT, while a 105mm howitzer projectile held 4.8lb. The 4.2in also provided more, though smaller, fragments than the 105mm.

THE VESSELS REMEMBERED

LCIs and LSMs were largely phased out after World War II by both the US Navy and Royal Navy. Few were used in the Korean War, but some fire support craft remained in operation through the Vietnam War and some were converted to specialized auxiliaries.

Only one each LCI(L)-351 class and LSM are displayed as memorials today – no fire support craft or other versions survive. There are a very few former LCIs still in commercial use, but they have been much altered. Most were scrapped over the years, including the majority of those turned over to other navies. Some were privately purchased and used as lighters, inshore cargo vessels, vehicle and passenger ferries, sightseeing boats, and even a floating restaurant.

LCI(L)-713 is displayed at the Amphibious Forces Memorial Museum, Vancouver, WA, and is maintained by the USS Landing Craft Infantry Association (http://www.usslci.com/index.html). LSM-45 is undergoing further renovation at Camp Lejeune's Mile Hammock Bay, Jacksonville, NC, by the Museum of the Marine (http://www.museumofthemarine.org/mcl.php) and the LSM/LSMR Association (http://lsmlsmr.org). Funding is not available and the ship is looking for a new home.

The stern of LSM(R)-401, the lead ship of the much redesigned and improved rocket ship. The stern kedge anchor and its rack are similar to those found on the LCI(L). This class did not see action in World War II, but eight were operational during the Korean War and three saw Vietnam service.

BIBLIOGRAPHY

Anon, *LSM-LSMR World War II Amphibious Forces*,
    Turner Publishing, Paducah, KY (1994)
Anon, *USS LCI*, Turner Publishing, Paducah, KY (1997
Baker II, A. D., *Allied Landing Craft of World War
    Two*, Naval Institute Press, Annapolis, MD
    (1985). (Originally published as *Allied Landing
    Craft and Ships*, ONI 226, 1944, with
    Supplement No. 1, 1945.)
Bruce, Colin J., *Invaders: British and American
    Experience of Seaborne Landings 1939–1945*,
    Chatham Publishing, London (1999)
Camp, Dick. *Iwo Jima Recon: The U.S. Navy at War*,
    February 17, 1945, Zenith Press, St Paul, MN
    (2007)
Friedman, Norman, *US Amphibious Ships and Craft:
    An Illustrated Design History*, Naval Institute
    Press, Annapolis, MD (2002)
Rielly, Robin L., *Mighty Midgets at War: The Saga of
    the LCS(L) Ships from Iwo Jima to Vietnam*,
    Hellgate Press, Central Point, OR (2000)

INDEX

References to illustrations are shown in **bold**.